I NEVER SCREAM

I NEVER SCREAM
New and Selected Poems

by
Pinkie Gordon Lane

LOTUS PRESS
Detroit

Copyright © 1985 by Pinkie Gordon Lane

First Edition
All rights reserved

International Standard Book Number 0-916418-58-8
Library of Congress Catalog Card Number 85-80139

Printed in the United States of America

Acknowledgment is gratefully made to the following publications in which some of these poems first appeared: *The Black Scholar; Callaloo; Confrontation; Deep Rivers; Discourses on Poetry; Energy West; Griefs of Joy; Hoo Doo 5; Jeopardy; Journal of Black Poetry; Ms.; The Mystic Female* by Pinkie Gordon Lane (South and West, Inc., 1978); *Negro American Literature Forum; The New Orleans Review; Nimrod; Obsidian; Pembroke Magazine; Poems by Blacks* (Vols. I, II, and III); *Poet; South and West; The Southern Review; Voices International;* and *Wind Thoughts* by Pinkie Gordon Lane (South and West, Inc., 1972).

Lotus Press, Inc.
Post Office Box 21607
Detroit, Michigan 48221

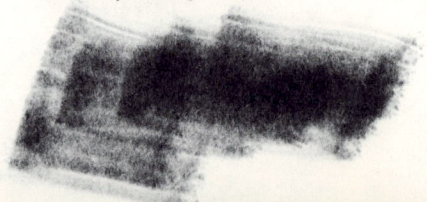

For Gordon

CONTENTS

I

Metaphors

Wind Thoughts 13
Midnight Song 14
Lake Murry 16
Waiting for April 9, 1984 17
Breathing 18
Leaves 19
Listenings 20
Rain Ditch 21
Migration 22
Two Poems 23
Waiting 24
A Quiet Poem 26
Yesterday's Sculptors 27
I Never Scream 28
Miscarriage 29
Roasting Grasshoppers 30
Opossum 31
Me 33
Four "Found" Poems 34
Baton Rouge Poems 36

II

People

Poems to My Father 43
To Singers of Song 48
Children 49
Elegy: Marion 50
To a Woman Poet That I Know 51
Three Bills 53
Four Poems for Gordon 54

(Continued)

Girl at the Window   57
Old Photo from a Family Album: 1915   58
Portrait   60
Letter   61
On Being Head of the English Department   62
When You Read This Poem   63
Sexual Privacy   64
Message   65
Dying (Poems for Ulysses Simpson Lane)   67

III

Love

Love Songs   77
Poem Extract   93
Love Considered   94
Silence   95
Letter   96
Three Love Poems   97
St. Valentine's Eve Poem   99
Mid-Summer Thoughts   100
Spring   101
While Sitting in the Airport Waiting Room   102
Love Poem   103
Survival Poem   104

"**Remember this: I never scream**"
(May Miller, "The Scream")

I
METAPHORS

WIND THOUGHTS

> ". . . the wind
> that led us here, the stillness in the air."
> *(Stanley Plumly)*

The wind led me here
and stillness holds me.

I might have asked
what caught my tightening throat,
why silence piled on silence
carries the weight of all my
years. Why I pause
on an afternoon and reach
for the color of wind.
(Wind does have color,
you know . . . yellow, I think,
with a touch of blue.)

Once I walked through the woods
with the abandonment of fall —
following a trail of leaves
till it led to an old house
covered with sky.
A door hung on one hinge
lying open like a ripped shirt.
Dragonflies sounded its depths
and swarming bees guarded the hall.
Had I been braver, I would have
planted my measured breathing
in the low sweep of its death
and settled in the mold
clustered on the steps like mice.

I shall return one day
to the light that nurtured
my youth, the city that once
held my mother's smile.
But I will surround myself
with the color of wind-days
and speak to the stillness
that follows thought upon thought
and touches my eyes like rain.

MIDNIGHT SONG

If I were sitting
on the banks of the river
I would write poems
about seaweed or flotsam
making their way
to the end of the sea
or the expanse of the bridge
that falls into the sky

If a flight to nowhere
curled waves of air
beneath my feet
or framed my vision, a poem
would draw images
from wings of the jet
filling corners of clouds

But my blue room —
where I die each night —
frames this poem
The curtain is striped
blue on white
the walls the color
of twilight just before death
of the sun
and the doors pale
as the morning sky

And so I write
a blue room poem
My mind penetrates walls
and hangs like mist
on the wake of trees
swaying low over the town

Only the crickets know
I am there, and they
sing songs
to the low-touching
wind   Only they
will know
I have passed over the earth
gathering periwinkles
and ivy
to take to the hills

This poem plants itself
and grows like the jasmine
coating my fence
It creeps over the page
like hollyfern
and bores into the depths
of my mind like the wild palm
that sentinels my yard's
center, spreading fan-like
at all points
caught up in a web
of light —
a ring of gold
painting the earth

LAKE MURRY

Sunset by the lake.
The evening molds
the opposite shore
(its angle of tree-lined banks
slanting downward)
and "The Point" — a thrust of land
maps the inlet
swallowed by sloping water.

A sailboat in the distance
juts upward like a shark's fin,

only the crickets
and the shaft of birds
flying down
moving counter to the incoming tide.
Sea grass along the shore
outlines the shallows,
patches of it as tall as a man
undisturbed
and a low wind
touching.

A flow into color loses itself
in the evening's low sweep,
anchors the stillness,
lights the dark undertow.
The gold rim of the lake
(no longer visible)
becomes a fusion of thought
and movement, pressing inward —
and breaking of mind
upon darkness and
tide.

WAITING FOR APRIL 9, 1984

Each moment rises into the
dark moon
and the days pass like thunder
One by one I meet each challenge
pausing only for breath
and fitful night sleeping —

I dare not surround myself
with silence
for then the heaviness would
drown me in space   And
no one would care more than
once   Then the days
would take on their usual fitness
and hours slow and measured
would be but a dream

I am dancing, dancing....
Did you know that flesh
and vision and spirit and
love are all the same?

BREATHING

There is an absolute quiet
in this house — as if the walls
were hugging the extremities
of their own darkness

One creak of the furnace
touches this silence
measuring the small
circle of blue
lining the perimeters
of this room

Settling back into my
special world of hushed
waiting, I know there are no
areas I've not touched
at some point in my life

The swelling of the brain
the shrinking of the heart —
all are familiar territory:
the explorer who has reached
the last frontier of time
of space,
a path of no
return

LEAVES

i

Year after year I watch
the way the compact dots
(miracles)
grow and take the shape
of soft Spring and Summer forms
large, inevitable
always independently withdrawn

I see them lean to the wind
without a thought of destiny,
social reform, taxes,
rent, or politics
without a thought even
of writing poems

Soon they will burn
up their green energy
will cover once again
my yard like cast-off
brown paper flags
I will gather them
in plastic bags, or pile
them in flower beds

ii

The first chill of autumn
will unlock the dark lonely anger, pulled
from the corners of my youth
from the daily resurrection of memory

I will crash into my golden burial
only to rise each morning
with renewed resolve
always making promises to myself
always plunging into the open air
an Olympian marathon runner
determined to race myself to
death

LISTENINGS

    "How much of yourself are you willing to risk?"
                                      (Jewel Prestage)

There are running feet
on my roof's top.
Mice? or squirrels?
Or perhaps only the ghost
of windfall. Why
do they hurry so — plunge
to the edge, then back
again, an endless frantic
game? Is it a chase
to beat the evening's chill?
A pursuit, or a death's race?
Or only sun, an urgent
need for fun to tilt
the scales?

Nothing now.
Only a shrill call
and the silence of night,
grumblings of a distant truck,
and a dog's bark. I count
the minutes. Wait.

Will the stillness reach
the level of pond's water?
Or carry me out to the
sea?

RAIN DITCH

We swam in the rain-filled gulley
one day
three black kids
unmindful of death's spectre:
water snakes
fever
cow dung floating like a drowned corpse,
the level of that ditch
our shoulders' height,
the water to our asses.

And just over the hill the weeds
bowed like cloistered nuns at vespers.
At eye distance just beyond,
our house's top formed a gray peak
against a crimson sky.

We remembered our fun for days,
talked about it,
longed for another torrent of rain
so that we could splash again in that
death trap.

MIGRATION

(For Clarence Marie Collier)

The winter birds
are flying from the North
to embrace our swamps
our rain-trapped fields/
My backyard trees hang
heavy and Louisiana
is a depot for this alien flock/
Their noisy forms slice the air
in restless flight
translated out of need/

The autumn mist mud-packs
the earth/ Caladiums,
their once firm stalks
reaching high, now bend
to snake the grass and wait
for death/ Hibiscus
forks the air to reach
the sky — a last count
before frost/ I know

the time to seek
new ground, when what
I wanted, felt, erupts
from leaning's desert ice/
flocks to a new Spring
and Southern warmth/

winter's frost a forgotten
land, and time a revolving
flame/

TWO POEMS

I

And finally the air
settles down to a comfortable
moist calm
the colors of day
mingled with edges
fading inward

and I, in my innocence,
swept into stone

I look into my garden
and filter the silence . . .
beautiful, deep, menacing

II

The garden-swing moves
back and forth   My son
has just sprung
from its center
to chase motion
An elm almost touches
the canopy   Two sycamores
grown together frame a cedar
fence
Filtered sunlight dots
the ground

It is as calm as death

WAITING

> "You may find peace and tenderness
> even in the center of the fiery winds."
> *(Dudley Randall, "Sanctuary")*

What if sound ceased
and waves of air
no longer volatile
suddenly became oceans
raging, raging,
a giant, moving wall

It is spring now: March
and the buds of leaves rush into form
The immanence of season
vaporizes thought
Mind has hardly time
to space itself

I am unsettled by silence
It is an echo
splitting the brain
penetrating hollows of eyes
creeping, creeping

Light frames itself around
the evening   The sun
mirrors in waters
Winds tremble in the bayous
rustling the stillness
polarizing edges of years

If I were wiser
I would grow horns —
antennas, rather —
and grope my way to the river
where living things
spin, spin
with the tide

A voice in me whispers:
*Structure the sunlight
form and pattern
Hold hands with the beauty
of Spring rain*

But I run with directed madness
into the green wild wood

waiting for something to happen
for trees to drop into holes
or sky to swallow tips of tongue
dancing on fire

A QUIET POEM

This will be a quiet poem.
Black people don't write
many quiet poems
because what we feel
is not a quiet hurt.
And a not-quiet hurt
does not call
for muted tones.

But I will write a poem
about this evening
full of the sounds
of small animals, some fluttering
in thick leaves, a smear
of color here and there —
about the whisper of darkness
a gray wilderness of light
descending, touching
breathing.

I will write a quiet poem
immersed in shadows
and mauve colors
and spots of white
fading into deep tones
of blue.

This is a quiet evening
full of hushed singing
and light that has no
ends, no breaking
of the planes, or brambles
thrusting out.

YESTERDAY'S SCULPTORS

"Should we forget the past? I don't think so."
(Ernest J. Gaines)
(For Charles H. Rowell)

Up on a hill on a windless day
I watch the year slip lowly
into a gray perspective —
a lingering folding of light.
The years pass quickly
like a riotous day in June
green and wild and lonely
and unbelievably laden
with stops and sound.
They harvest a rise and a fall —
rage silently.

Voices cry from the bayous
windfall rousing the deaf
and the dead, listeners of sorrow.
Stillness touches the night
breathing on lynched men
wedded to swollen trees.

And the women —
the women survive
and grow tall and straight.

I listen for sound
of memory, reach into the past
fondle the relics
the fragments of color and pain
the segments of joy
molding me into my today
framing my tomorrow.

    Shall we forget the past?
    I don't think so.

I NEVER SCREAM

> "Remember this: I never scream"
> *(May Miller, "The Scream")*

The hour draws its own design
on this thin atmosphere
floating like lint outside my window.

That quick black pattern
of branches abstracts
the green canvas of leaves.
And the puddle at the base
spacing the ground
in spots of sky-reflected light
lacks the depth to shape
my mind.

I have a locked-in psyche,
leather-padded, hinged,
opening up and thrusting out
only when I choose
to make it so.

I am weather bound
insulated
cooled by laminated shadows
closing out harshness
locking in brief hushed
colors of sound.

I see the patterns
as they design
the not impetuous night.
Do they reach the point
where space meets space
where twilight spans the mind
in one broad thrust —
a warm, soft band
melting, flowing,
gone?

MISCARRIAGE

I share this clot of blood with you,
This pulse of life
Drenched with a dripping, throbbing beat,
Softly flowing like the tears of Niobe.

    I share this life so early turned to death.
    I share this non-birth, wrenched of quickened breath.

ROASTING GRASSHOPPERS

Roasting grasshoppers meant
making
an oven out of fist-sized
rocks clustered together
like the petals
of a rose bud,
dropping
the live grasshopper inside,
topping
our oven with a flat stone,
building
a fire underneath.

The grasshopper
exchanged his suit
of mud green for a brilliant
toasted red.

We then tossed
him in the grass
under a tulip leaf
for the robins to find
or for the carrion ants
to haul away and cache
for winter's food.

OPOSSUM

This visitor to my patio
thinks he is
unobserved. Going
from plate to plate
he sniffs for scraps
left by pets who do not seek
him.

> *Who will write a poem*
> *about you, your body round*
> *as a bottle, and nose extended*
> *with unacknowledged grace?*

I open the door. He leaves
without hurry. Caution
rather than fear measures
his departure. I wait . . .
respecting his distance
his knowledge of finalities
that end even before they begin.

> *Who will write a poem*
> *about you, when there are wars*
> *to be fought, and people*
> *yet to die in the streets,*
> *their bodies wasted to*
> *elements?*

Bombs splinter the air
and children reach for a crust
of bread, their eyes melting inward
like new-fallen snow.
Cry! for the women who are raped

(Continued)

even while the sun casts streaks
of red in the eastern
sky . . .

A poem about an unlovely
beast — an anachronism?

Sanity reaches for balance
and rests on this visitor
exploring, unhurried —
accepting without question
today's pastel falling
into evening's quiet final
death.

ME

If I could remember back to when
I was an embryo . . .
I probably wondered even then
what queer sauce went into the making
of me —
an odd bunch of wind and straw,
rose water and crushed ice,
a mite, a worm,
a demon-coated, bright-eyed hawk.

And I scrouged against the brick wall
of Edgely Street
sidling like a crab —
shy with strangers
to whom, when friends,
I in reverse became the tyrant,
issuing directives with a particular skill —
and loved too much for my own good
baring the target of my flesh
like a silly bird too tame to fly
too wild to trust to fondling.

I swept down into cellars of thought
and taxed a throbbing brain,
an electric heart,
bursting and bursting through pink walls
and climbing the dust of earth.

Chilling screams were my lullaby.
But in spite of all,
I elongated like a salt water taffy
and claimed my portion
not understanding
but borne by instinct to the stars,
and holding not unseemly.

FOUR "FOUND" POEMS

I. Strategic Site

>(*State Times*, Baton Rouge, February 20, 1984, p. 1-A)

They abandoned their positions
by midmorning
to board landing craft
headed for naval vessels
off shore

A spokesman said some
would remain on ships
and some would sail home
Some members of the contingent
would remain on shore
as a "clean-up" crew

But they had not yet
received orders to start
troop redeployment
Evacuees said "Nothing
is going on"

Warplanes on Sunday
hit guerrilla bases
in the central mountains

"Peacekeeping" forces then
withdrew

II. Combat Zone

>(*Time*, February 20, 1984, p. 34)

As darkness fell, the combat
grew in the savage street
Afraid of what the night
would bring, many sought
refuge   Every minute
seemed to bring the sounds of
rockets   Even the usual

wail of crisis could not be
heard

Fire trucks did not risk
making runs

III. Strangers

> (*The Morning Advocate*, Baton Rouge,
> February 20, 1984, pp. 1-A, 6-A)

Monty and Julie died the night
of September 23, each with a bullet
in the head   They were found
on the seat of a new Datsun
parked near a city housing project

The car's ceiling light was
burning   A white poodle
was on Julie's lap

Shooting is a way to fill
an afternoon   The fear
of crimes of violence
is not just a fear of injury
or death

It is a fear of strangers

> I sleep with the light
> on now

IV. Technology

> (*State Times*, Baton Rouge, February 20,
> 1984, p. 12-A)

A subway train broke free
of its moorings today
and rolled through eight
underground stations

The iron chain anchoring
it to the rails came loose
It was not known how
the anchor broke

An investigation was
ordered

BATON ROUGE POEMS

i

Baton Rouge #1

Horizontal
this city spreads herself
like a great cat sprawled
in the sun.

Her sounds are sponged into
the overhanging sky
that measures her dimensions
by tips of sweet gums
breaking the horizon,
by tar-black smoke
(from its monstrous oil plant)
belched from fierce
hissing streaks
of orange fire.

Sweet rain-soaked air
drips into her belly's
felt need
and the summer's sun
vaporizes the tears
of her ever-present
poor.

Traveling by car transports
to green plains
and purple bayous:
cypresses moss-strung
and drooping to wedged base
split by gray waters
· carrying the face of day
and cradling the stillness
of nights.

The city spins . . .
simulating metropolis
flops back on her boneless
tail
and purrs herself
to ambience.

ii

Baton Rouge #2

I have come down
from the hills today

down into the valley
this gutted street
of the city

They are building an expressway
a sure sign of progress
I am told
The red earth is turned up
like potato rows in New Jersey

and the steel rods
stand one by one
waiting to be pillared
and braced

I am writing poems
in this breathing space

A cry in the distance
tells me visions are
not in vain

(Continued)

iii

What It Is Like Living in Baton Rouge

This city is a political pool
lending itself to ferment
and noise, to terrifying silences...
to light around the corner
sifting through windows, doors,
through quiet places.

One can stand at a distance
and see magnolias bending
to the ground, women in doorways
with babies for bracelets.
The ambience of crickets
and racing motor cars fills
the air, and the smell
of rain, the pungent odor
from the huge oil plant
hangs everywhere.

It is a city without skyscrapers,
walls without keepers —
people, people circling for
space. The city moves
like a giant caterpillar —
North to South, East to West,
while the Mississippi snakes
its way under the overhanging
bridge.

Living in Baton Rouge is like
living in the hollow of nowhere.
It is like disappearing into the
night, like darkness, like sun,
like beauty, like song,
like knowing you are
surrounded only by your "self,"
touched only by your own skin,
like pouring your loneliness
into a great pool of
light.

iv

Kaleidoscope: Leaving Baton Rouge

The music comes to me
from all corners of the room
stereo turned up in volume
to the fullness of space
surrounding me

Cleansed, purged
exorcised to silence
I slip into the valleys
of my mind, fused
to a green landscape

> The river is calm today
> Only the great purple shadow
> of the towering bridge
> moves with the Mississippi

I have come obliquely
from the North where the snows
cover the fields of New Jersey
and the brown stones of Pennsylvania

> Now lingering in the backwaters
> of Louisiana bayous
> I am ghost, spirit, woman
> exploring the mirrors of my mind
> prisms of light caught in the undertow

The trick is to avoid
smashing into myself

I think I hear
the mist falling
The sound of it captures me
even more than the purple-gray
haze it makes of the dawn

Its frequency says:
> *Breathe*

(Continued)

V

Southern University

(Baton Rouge, Louisiana)

I walk in the morning light
This campus is deserted now
except for one bird
hung low in a slow current
of chill air

Hidden behind trees
near a place where three graves
wait in dark stillness
the Mississippi moves — a gray
sheet of glass with no sound

The college stands   It is
an ascending ladder
that does not guarantee joy
or fill the hour before
death

Movement is broken
as torn leaves
catch the morning draft
One small brown mouse traces
a path to the earth-breathing
banks

Silence touches my skin
And no one comes
to beckon me down

When will the sun follow
my eyes
and curve to the dark bend
of the river?

II
PEOPLE

POEMS TO MY FATHER

> "and in the low light
> coming out of the hill
> he is his own darkness"
> *(Stanley Plumly)*

i. Introduction

You used to ricochet
down the street at evening
time — breath reeking
and loose, and
body lumbering,
finely precarious.

Oh Papa! This legacy
is metal. But
I cannot be your savior.
Time and distance raze you —
a Ulysses wandering
fate-driven out of the universe
but forever in the heart.

You — timelessly circling
in my dark.
Dim-hued
yet bright
an endless cord binding
me to past and present
and who knows what
future suns and season.

ii. Walking the Dog

We entered the dark house
that day, Papa,
do you remember?
The odor of gin and corn bread
incongruously mixed
and the lap-lap sound
feet of our big German Shepherd
("King", we called him)

(Continued)

his long gentle claws scraping the floor
the two of us
trailing like forgotten lovers
and you strode like a giant
swaggered with your hand
in your pocket

back to the ailing kitchen,
walls creaking with age-dust
the linoleum floor cracked
and scaled like a land-flattened
sea fish.

(It was our final odyssey,
Circe's isle revisited)

A short trip up the back stairs
an exchange even shorter
(a pint of white lightning for silver
coins)
the look of chagrin when you turned
and caught my eye
your post-scripted warning
to silence . . .

and I melted into the dark
like a stranger stalking the
shadows.

iii. Epileptic

You trembled like an egg,
rolled over backwards
and died,
Father from whose loins I sprang.

Your disease was only part
of your dismissal, you
who had been going for a long time.

Your perfumed breath
reached down into the hell
of you
wrapping your flesh
like a bundle
the cord ever tightening
till it cut beyond blood and bone.

And I felt your quivering pain
numbing and thawing your jellied
eye
and you cursing the gods
that made you.

iv. Sequel No. 1

I said you cursed the gods
that made you. And the
white belly of a fish
ransacked your brain
leaving it floating
in the film of sea.

"Inez you bitch"

ran triads of hateful love
flowing from your hot
bowels churned by torment
of what devils? Whose spikes
did you pitch after your day
of lumber at the docks?
Whose bricks capsized
your skin and lumped
the flowing of your blood?

"Inez you bitch"

the hardened crust of stone
spans your hurt
and rises from the plot
that holds your box
of silk.

(Continued)

v. Sequel No. 2

And besides,
you were my father
and I loved you fiercely —
disgust, anger, love — all
lumped together
while I defied those who
would malign you.
I pitied you, too —
poor wild, sad, raging
creature who had forgotten
how to love
whose flesh had turned to worms
and whose breath was a song
of death.

vi. Sequel No. 3

I meant to tell you this, Papa,
I've divorced myself
from your memory.
The years never happened...
only the times when we
laughed
and strolled through the York Street Park
your sweaty shirt
and owl-shaped pants
caught up in the wind.

The trembling jaw and glassy eye
(pale mirages). The
foaming of your blood and
tears that never formed,
gathering like dark clouds.
Your skull melting
in the hollow of my hands
while I waited to grow up.
The years dissolving into a stream of
darkness and your face
a spectre
of the mind.

You never happened,
Papa.
You were a shadow,
a low light,
a lost love
folding into the oval
of your night.

TO SINGERS OF SONG

      (For Frances Marsh Ellis)

Stay beautiful
with your strength
and your towering bronze
voice
lighting the sky
where a curtain of darkness
would hide us

Lest we forget, we
were not meant to rage
and weep alone
not even to flee
like the lost mad dog
in the wilderness

Even when we wither
in the spirit's faint cry
the bright jewels of the gifted
remind us of this:

    the dust of earth
    does not bind us
    nor will the worm dictate
    the mandate of flesh
    We will find a voice
    in the winds that sing in the fields —
    in the shaft of light that halts
                      bitterness
    And like the last leaf of autumn
    we will not forget the spring

CHILDREN

In the mid-dark of early night
we talked about how babies
were made, or came into the world.
We went to the barn
and shot pigeons with our
slingshots, watching them flutter
like frightened children
and drop like half-ripe apples
in a windstorm.

The really crowning times
came when we tormented
Aaron, shutting him out
of the lockets of our love
and watched him squirm
like a dismembered June Bug —
yearning for us to let him in
while we turned the key
and slid the latch
that forever sealed him out.

His revenge was perfect:
he turned his ass
to family
stole tires off cars
spit on our proud name
and embraced the
penitentiary . . .
spilling his own light
like a plunging star . . .

ELEGY: MARION

I.

Marion
(the addition of our years
barely the sum of fourteen)
you studied toe dancing
and ballet
with a slim brown form
elastic as a mouse,
resilient as a showered summer's day.

I remember you as a child remembers
first loves:
words unmarred by bittersweet,
the dark mystery of music,
the unpredictable spring of laughter.

Knowing you was an awakening
for me sprung from bats' wings,
root of hemlock, and blood of ice.

II.

You lay there small and dry and nineteen
reduced to an equation of chemicals and form.

I hastened from that death place
desecrating memory,
away from the smell of sickening sweet,
the too proper atmosphere
of chrysanthemums and wreath,
out into the shadowed mist

>to rose-dust filtering in the summer's light
>and gossamer spun obliquely in the night.

TO A WOMAN POET THAT I KNOW

i

When you lie again
in the street of forgetfulness
smashed beyond recognition
courting the dark avenue,
when you wake to the alien
walls that do not touch
your battered flesh
     your other self
       will fall into the locket
     of your mind and wait
     for truth

A creature without roots
standing on the brink
of private ruin,
your voice will not save you
for you have found the power
of destruction
     I weep for your lost
      self that stands on the edge
     of the terrible wood
     whose darkness draws

(Continued)

ii

If I could I would make
a gift: the magic of souls
spinning in the great center
that place where love meets
merged in the light

I would dispel your personal
and private hell
you, woman: black, lovely
and lost
you, poet
whose voice cries out
to the silent air
that dissolves you
      This elegy, this inscription
      becomes the dichotomy,
      the oxymoron, the paradox,
      the beauty, the strength
      of your existence,
      the destiny of this earth

THREE BILLS

Three Bills I knew.

One faded like a shadow
trading saxophone for
the last call of the night
owl's cry.

The other exchanged
light for love, and
brightness for a human touch.

And you, Bill,
will you hold the wind
against the edge of day
your strength and warmth
tucked in the morning's
shifting light?

FOUR POEMS FOR GORDON

I. South Paw Baby

    (at age six months)

I tried to make you right-handed soon,
But you couldn't find your mouth with the spoon.

II. Black Diamond

    (at age fifteen)

The kids are practicing rock —
"BLACK DIAMOND" they call
themselves   My living room
comes alive

How do I describe the sounds
that I hear?   Voices,
laughter, music, drums,
a medley caught in the trauma
of life

a waiting
a dividing of space
a reaching for the longitude
      wantonly pulling the poles
      that measure the ends
      of earth

Their private hells suspended . . .

III. Gordon

    (at age twenty-one)

              Now
a man   His jazz
a flight to magic
soaring with a downbeat
progressive, cool, funky

His appearance conservative
This boy four generations away
from slaves of the dormant
fields

              His drums
beat a vocal message
He "gigs" his way into
his own world and circles
angels, devils, with African
telecommunications in this
modern idiom

Gordon, my manchild,
grown to mid-proportions —
his silences tracking the
dawn

IV. Rite of Passage

     (at age twenty-one and a half, moving away from
     home into his own apartment)

Moving up, out, into
your own orbit
you tell me about Steinbeck's
"Flight" — and you quote
"rite of passage"
What is that, I ask

You say it is the "right"
to move into your own,
to define your own space,
to grow into the sunlight
of your own cranial sphere,
the shadow of your
walk through time
and music
Your own sadness —
to measure that distance —
your own dance
articulated with the drumbeat
of your heart

(Continued)

rite of passage — we
each have as a legacy
of growing up and daring
to challenge the terrible
beauty of our own alienation
our own walk in space
our own weightlessness
in a world of spiralling
centrifugal force — a race
to the unknown —

a rite of passage

GIRL AT THE WINDOW

She sits there,
hand on cheek, head
turned towards the open window
where shadows pulsate
like quivering beasts

Summer and autumn
contend in blue skies
and spiraling air —
ghosts and green light
a mere breath touching

A golden animal streaks
across space
and lavender hills outline
the rim

Will they tell
the level of seasons?
Will they fly home
to the sky?

    Her skin is copper-toned
    and eyes the nests
    of birds   She
    dreams of Nairobi
    and wildebeests

    the equator a blue line
    slung in mid-air

OLD PHOTO FROM A FAMILY ALBUM: 1915

(For Inez Addie West Gordon
and Ocydee Williams)

This lovely young woman,
with the elegant hat
and dress of flowing gauze,
sits in a chair (a rocker)
contemplating a feather
poised in two fingers
of her right hand

What photographer arranged
this photo in a studio
with the tapestried background
draped like a mural? See
how he catches
the pensive gaze,
face soft, unsmiling,
full of innocence and hope.

She sends the picture
to her lover:

> *Dear William, again*
> *I make another attempt*
> *— Please send me*
> *one of yours . . . or*
> *else you can come*
> *and make one*
> *at our house*

Her body curved, relaxed, slender —
the eyes returning into themselves
She is contained in her
assurance that leads
into the future

Nothing in this photo
resembles the gross figure
the angry defiance
the abused spirit
of the woman I knew

The enlarged hand,
fingers swollen from years of work,
would no longer hold a bird's feather
but a torch to light
her way back to corridors
of love expected
of fury diffused to a spiral
of smoke, and a gown
that (shroud of her life)
she might have placed
upon her unmarked
grave

PORTRAIT

He could release
the swelling
in his ribs
by crushing furniture
and hurling it to
hell
could curse till his face
bulged like a potato.

All else failing
to ease the white rage
scorching his brain
he'd get his shotgun
and send his dogs
(sometimes one, two, three,
or four at a time)
howling to dog-heaven.

At age fifty-two he died
drying up
like a piece of dehydrated beef.
The wind
blew him away
like a feather.

The last time I saw
him, tears glistened
in his eyes; his mind was
a twisted cork
that could not plug up
the bowels
of his brain.

LETTER

>"it is midnight
>no magical bewitching
>hour for me"
>   *(Sonia Sanchez, "poem at thirty")*

Sonia, you beautiful
black sister who
knows how to sing
about your blackness —
these lines are for you.

We share a common bond:
>   For me, too,
>   "midnight" is "no
>   magical bewitching hour."
>   And I do not wish to be
>   "among strangers."

But

>   "Coming home" to me has
>   been the discovery that

>   love is greater than hate.

My black beauty is inviolable.
I know this, and I smile
and walk straight and proud
with the knowledge
with the positive assurance
that we are tall
endowed with a humanity
that cannot be destroyed
through oppressive tyranny.

>   We can make our songs transcend sorrow.

We can penetrate the mist
of ignorance, ugliness, and pain

>   and create beauty out of love.

We have the gift of wholeness,
Sonia.

>   Let us sing.

ON BEING HEAD OF THE ENGLISH DEPARTMENT

I will look with detachment
on the signing of contracts,
the ordering of books,
and making of schedules —
will sing hymns of praise
to the negative, when
it is necessary, to survive.

    And if the morning
    light freezes in the east,
    a dawn-covered eye
    will tell me I am cold
    to your pleas, but never whore
    to the spirit. I will
    write poems in the blue-
    frosted lake.

If I disdain poetasters,
announcers, and the gods
of mediocrity, knowing
that they too insist on living,
it is because I hand you
the bread and the knife
but never the music and the art
of my existence.

You will not swallow me or absorb me:
I have grown too lean for that.
I am selfish, I am cruel,

    I am love.

WHEN YOU READ THIS POEM

(For Citizens Opposed to Censorship, Baton Rouge)

The earth turns
like a rainbow
And the smell of autumn
drifts down — yellow
leaf on my arched back

The light touches
I see it with my skin,
feel it lean
That furrow of trees
casts its shadow — long
as the night, the wind,
the river
Truth has many faces
My friends, don't honor me
without passion
I will not be
wheat in the summer's fire
I will not lie fallen
like autumn fruit
or die in the evening sun

Listen,
let us ban together
and fight evil   We
cannot let it burn
the earth   We
cannot let it guide
the sun

The world is a bird
in flight

When you read this poem,
love me

SEXUAL PRIVACY

The ACLU Mountain States Regional Office came across a welfare application used in . . . [a certain state] for women with illegitimate children. Among the questions:

— When and where did you first meet the defendant [the child's father]?
— When and where did intercourse first occur?
— Frequency and period of time during which intercourse occurred?
— Was anyone else ever present? If yes, give dates, names, and addresses.
— Were preventive measures always used?
— Have you ever had intercourse with anyone other than the defendant? If yes, give dates, names and addresses.

(*The Privacy Report*, American Civil Liberties Union Foundation, Vol. IV, No. 3, Oct., 1976.)

When and where did you first
confront loneliness?
When and where did you resist
the urge to die?
Did you pull a blind around
your sorrow?
Was anyone present? If yes, give
names and dates and addresses.
Did you survive?
Were preventive measures always used?
Who listened to the rage of your
silent screams? Give the frequency
and period of time,
dates and names and addresses . . .

Will you promise never to breathe ice?
To follow the outline
of a city street whose perspective
darkens with the morning light?

Document.

MESSAGE

> (To the brother who thinks poets should stop writing;
> National Conference of African-American Writers,
> Washington, D.C., 1974)

I have found my voice
in the attic
in the silence of closed rooms
in the night winds raging
I am a stranger
a thief who follows sound
with ears

Mama's knees no longer hurt
for they have grown an outer skin
and her wooly hair
is pinned back at the neck
One by one she watched her loves
turn to dust: music
color, poetry

I listen to rain —
its deep tones
like night air after supper
when voices run faster
than thoughts
or children playing in the streets

Lovers, gather your bones
Don't let them vanish
in spaces
Listen

(Continued)

   Listen,
we cannot be without grace
like those who have forgotten
love

My friends, listen,
I cannot take from you
more than I give
Did you think I would
diminish you?

   Hear
the beating of hearts
in the harvest of music
whose song is a message
is life
Listen

    Listen

DYING

(Poems for Ulysses Simpson Lane)

I. Slumbering Bats

Death lies over this house
like an emaciated giant
uncertain as to where to rest
his hoary head.
I look cross-eyed at
blossoms dropping in the sun
hanging like slumbering bats.

        Spring has a way
of stumbling in like an
inebriated old man. I cling
to living things — a kitten
in a furry ball at my feet,
shepherd dogs that rumble
like steam engines,
a pot of flowers (skinny
old maids climbing vine-like,
a wall's shadow, reaching
aimlessly with crooked fingers).

        Old men marry
young girls half their age
in self-denial of
the broken cage . . .
I surround myself with life
and watch bellies
fatten like earthworms,
bulge like happy pigs —
dumb brutes
positive in their blindness
that they will live forever

(Continued)

II. Finis #1

The plane's motor roars
like a forest fire
Wings spread eagle, boxed
high over a sprawling scroll
of land
It is his dying day
his millennium
Hell's exit

I sit and listen to the sounds of talking
Someone is eating
Coughing scratches the dim silence beyond
The motor now becomes platitude
The sign on the wing says
"no step"
and the throb in my flesh
beats "no step," "no entrance"

It is the journey past thought

III. Finis #2

See how the jasmine
leans to the sky.
A blue/pink petal
selects a space of air
to hide the ominous
shadow of death

I lean forward, smell
the sour/sweet odor
of summer rain caught
just beneath the frilled
edges of clustered blooms

Beyond this space, this
effusion of color,
the pale glow of twilight
spreads beneath
the crimson
sky

(Continued)

IV. Songs to the Dialysis Machine

dedication

Being woman, I
write this poem
with the voice of the woman.
But it is for you, Pete,
man with the proud hate
and the circling eyes.
Curse the posture of the chair!
Spit on it! The bastard
mummy hours. Yet
remember: the cold, still
blood and the paralytic
limbs would now be legend
were it not for the
machine.

i. introduction

Nobody knows
what a dialysis machine is,
really,
or cares.
They think
the artificial kidney
is something sewn up
inside you
and works like a clock
or a programmed
computer.

ii. the dialysis machine called the artificial kidney

Where life is a luxury
and death a dark dream.

It sucks the life-flowing
blood
and sends it back
as a promised gift.

Red flowing through clear
plastic tubes
like God's river —

this miracle of man's mind.

iii. leg cannulas* for the dialysis machine

A rubber stamp day. The sun
as usual a golden spider
creeping to the top of the sky.

Dropping a bottle of cologne
on my foot
of small import, as a rule,
now becomes a Grendel.
My leg gorges herself with bruised
blood and laughs
herself to spikes and needles.
Cannulas clot.
I race against time
to deft fingers for irrigating
veins.
Bleeding is a luxury
I pray for.

iv. the hum of the dialysis machine

This humming does not have
the hum of birds
nor is it like the wildly
soft wind.
It does not cup the evening shade
in rock-swollen fields.

Artless, unbroken, without sex
or mind,
it measures life by inches
and is sweet.

*Two plastic tubes inserted under the skin, in the arm or
  leg, one being attached to the artery, the other to the vein.
  These are connected to the arterial and venous tubes of the
  dialysis machine.

(Continued)

If this humming stops
my life will ebb like the tide
without grace or beauty
though I cling in puzzled anger
to this iron sheath
of day.

v. mood

And since each day is a long shadow
stretching the evening,
I let the river of my mind
flow freely.

Each act of will
(courting indecision,
courting death)
rides the four winds converging
in a massive
whirlpool of amber light.
Each day lies suspended
beneath unhinged
loops of rope.

Unsmiling time
unbeating hearts
ungrasping hands
slide round the yellow wind
and bolts slip out of place
beneath the sun

vi. back again

I fight for life
and put my whole weight
against the door of death.
Stubbornly I cling
to this semi-brightness
this facade of existence.

The vagueness of "unsmiling time"
becomes a clock-hour day
measured in minutes and seconds.
I see in reverse
all the passing years.

"Live one day at a time,"
they tell me. "Let the future
take care of itself."
Can one corner time
and seal it in a jar
like a bottled insect?

The day is not suspended now
but is a block of ice
beneath my feet.
Each frozen hour
waits for spring
and the melting season.

(Continued)

III
LOVE

LOVE SONGS

i. awakening

It is time for a poem.
I know the time
when sleepless nights and beating
    of the heart
ring tones of troubled mind —
vague, like an off-shore hollow voice,
deep, deep as the light in your eyes,
Love.

It is time for a poem —
diamond-cased and unapproachable things,
sinewed-strung.

(Dare I sing this song?)

Once I was so sure of what was
right and what was wrong,
could have laid down golden rules
that say: "This is the line
one must not cross —"
How beautiful, and simple.
How uncomplex.

Darkness gathers brightly
and my demon starlets dance
like tinseled ghosts on a saint's night.

Don't speak to me of what is wrong
or right —
your law voices and your Janus faces —
In my heart I know:
right is what hurts others least.

(Continued)

My human frailness plunges
in blossoms of the Spring
and drowns in the ocean's
sweet and pungent depths —

This poem is for you, oh sweet,
oh selfless, tender,
unassuming friend —

my love.

ii. what does one say to the mad?

> "What does one say to the mad? They hang
> from their trees like swollen fruit, unwilling
> to fall..."   *(Charles Wright)*

What does one say to the mad?
To the mad hate, the mad pain,
the mad, mad love?

Listening shadows glance off the wall,
hiding past my mad new day —
What does one say to this mad new love,
Love?
Tell me.

iii. despair

> "The day of my soul is
> the nature of that
> place. It is a landscape. Seen
> from the top of a hill."
>   *(LeRoi Jones)*

Love,
the top of the hill is
the lower waiting place
of my days and nights. The
day of my soul sings darkly
like the crickets in
the swollen grass.

It is hopeless, yes.
And I curse my mind's lament —
so silly and so foul.

The iron gate hangs slantingly,
neither letting in nor letting out.

Once I hid in an alcove
and let the night air
filter past my screaming eyes
shut against the wind.

The days are warmer now.
And I see your face
glowing like the sun.

The mirror hurls back
the falling day pulling
down the sky.
I sit and listen
to the stillness of my lips,
then murmur like a crazy bastard
drunk with wine.

The night canvasses
the howling of my bursting
flesh,
and nothing stops this idiotic reverie,
this song's lament.

iv. beyond words

Flesh
has a way
of reaching out
past pawns, tricks,
sophistication

an articulation
beyond compare.

(Continued)

All my words now seem
but the babblings
of an idiot
before the eloquence
of flesh
that speaks a poem
in the darkness
glancing off the soft light
creeping past our limbs
and soaking up
the night.

v. for a future's treasury

> "... we feel enough left there
> In our commotion to stir the spirit
> As well as the flesh."   *(Carl Bode)*

The spirit and the mind, yes — a prelude
an overture. Our gliding on the lawn,
folding in tufts of grass.

Music tumbling in drifts
of wind
and a spilled sky dropping threads of
water in a summer's light.

Your smile was etched against the sun
with rays ricocheting across my fluttering pulse:
manna for the spirit —
our weaving webs of memory
stored for a future's treasury ...

And LOVE on an afternoon
balanced firmly on the days
of heart locked in our own
private place.

vi. "Write me a poem."

And yet there were times
when sun turned to willows,
light burned to ashes,
and I melted like a candle —
the night exploding darkly.

One word, one look, one smile —
and DAY
opened up like magic —
a sea of blinding light.

Tumbling in orbit,
I did not fall in love:
I flowed into it
gently, firmly pulled —
my own volition
notwithstanding.

vii. for you

A brisk walk
on a half-cold
September day
and suddenly
a breeze capering
against the back
of my hand.

I loved you like
a sudden wind.
Bright-eyed fear and
wonder
tossed in the dark —
warm, edged with
sleeplessness and
disbelief.

(Continued)

"We cannot be all
of everything to one another,"
you said. Dear,
I know.
Neither can the rain
drain rivers
or sun stir sleepers
from the pit —

We cannot be all
of everything —
but let the
fragments be jewels
of light
and embers glowing
in the dark,
and love a catalyst
against an endless, aching
night.

viii. vignettes

(Suddenly)
there you were,
your voice
reaching out to me
over layers of
loneliness
and years of space.
        * * *

(Reality)
has a hard
cruel surface. At home
I face his cynic voice,
his sardonic, crisp
glittering words of hate.
And I run like hell
to escape his rage of
fear —
his hard round cage of
ice.
        * * *

("I love loving you,"
you said.)
A liaison of
feeling stretched
across the highways
of our
minds.

      * * *

(Mood) —
Shifting vessels
bending with
each day's demise,
merging into the
design of things
like forms on
an artist's
canvas.

      * * *

(My fear) —
Nothing
lasts forever . . .
not love
nor hate
nor need, desire
fire
ice.

      * * *

(What drew me to you?)
An impishness?
A devilish sparkle
of the eye?

There is a glow about you
a vitality
a boyishness
an unbelievable kindness
a humane empathy
a glorious enclosing spirit of
love.

      * * *

(Continued)

(We are)
lost
in the space of Time —
Singing like
Spring robins.
Dying like shadows
in the evening.
Holding like rain.
A breath away from
the sun's edge —
dangling on the fringe
of night.

ix. waiting out the days

We don't want the days
to become staple
like jelly or bread.

Let our knowing one another
be excitement
white passion
palpitation of the pulse
and all those things
that make our loving
a streak of lightning
an extraordinary thing.

Even agony
is better than boredom
and uncertainty
a tower over dull predictability . . .

Wouldn't you say?

x. communication

Let us
    not
  lose
the voice

that holds us
together.

No magical string
holds the heart.
Like any vital organ
it has logical
connections — vessels
leading in and leading
out.

Nothing from nothing
leaves nothing
and a vacuum is only itself...

The voice
is our heart's
vessel

Love.

xi. coffee hour

carried me miles and miles off-shore.
Once I tried floating back
like a dead fish.
I even tried swimming.
The best thing to do
is to lay the belly flat
and drink the waves,
merging with land and sea and sky —
sound frequency submerged
in light and blending with the air...

You were there, your flesh
wrapped in shirt and tie and tweed.
Coffee singed my lips
and I sighed contentedly.

(Continued)

xii. shadows

Danger follows like a lurking shadow.
It seeps around and over and under.
Once I thought I saw his form
trailing like a malignant seeker
after what is lost —
forever gone.
What does he hope to gain?
Does he think to resurrect ghosts
of the past? To chain
a spirit?
What gravity does he think
will pull us down together to the suction earth?

Does he believe we will rise like angels
and sweep away the shit years?
Or does he suppose they never happened?

>   Fool!
>   Don't you know that nothing
>   remains the same?
>   And that the line between us
>   grows interminably long?
>   And that any direction at all
>   is better than none?

xiii. griefs of joy

No, nothing remains the same.
And my spirit reaches out to you
my love
without apologies
without embarrassment
with only the thought that this is
right for us
that moving towards you is like
touching leaves in autumn
or reading Yeats and Cummings
together on a special night —
my chin grazing your neck
as you glide through
my father moved through dooms of love

while "our sames of am and haves of give"
give measures of light drifting
through our "griefs of joy,"
our minds and spirits
interlocked like death.

The splendor of the moment
moves quietly, softly, calmly
without fuss or bother
to some point of unforgetfulness
and love.

xiv. loving

Looped in each other's arms
without thought of ending,
we are sure only
of the reality of the moment.
Morals is a private affair,
and "hell," said Faustus,
"is but a fable."

To avoid banality, we lock
the silence in,
with only low tones of the record player
moaning irrelevant music — sounds
sucked into the low light
seeping through the half-drawn shades.

Let's not rush towards
our own destruction.

This moment's dying cauterizes death
and breathes life into the sinews
strung together.

(Continued)

xv. a backward look

> "We in love skate
> over the knuckles of others."
> *(Joyce Carol Oates)*

without meaning to, of course,
but it is inevitable.
Light descends
and blindingly blanks the path.
We are diffused into all of it.
We try evaluating this
and weighing that —
are sure we are being quite intelligent
                about it all.
But when the passage clears a little
we see trickles of blood
staining the back trail.
"The knuckles were in the way,"
we say.
No, not really. We
just refused to see them.

xvi. apprehension

I am cold sometimes
and tremble.
I am afraid — not of the dark
or even of the half-demolished shade
but only of the possibility
of the terrible, terrible
void
that in the wake
you will be gone
that the structured years
descending
will engulf you.

I live now only for each day
overwhelmed by every moment.
The future is a dim harbor
that I don't even try to
fathom.

xvii. finis

Should this final poem
be sad?
But it is not
and what I feel for you
is whole, and
real
a moving in and out
of the beauty of you —
a private joy of
knowing you and
growing
into you.

It is time to stop the lines.
But love lives on.

> My human frailness plunged
> in blossoms of the Spring
> and drowning in the ocean's
> sweet and pungent depths —
> These poems are for you, oh sweet,
> oh selfless, tender
> unassuming friend —
>
> my love.

xviii. postscript

("I would rather be beautifully happy.")

And there is no finality —

My home was in your smile
and in the darkness
of your voice —
Each day a pendant
between love and pain.

I —
selfish
in my enclosing
grasping
the loosening threads . . .

(Continued)

This final word — the hour
of knowing that only with light
and air can we survive.
The ashes now lie softly
on the ground.

You have taught me
the meaning of being
finally, beautifully . . .
sad.

xix. sunrise

I don't try now to push
the days into corners.
I watch the leaves
drift like feathers
and listen for the sound
of you in windfall.
I see your eyes in patches
of blue spotted through the trees
like wet paint on my canvas,
your smile hanging loosely
in my mind's recess.

An oriole flits to the ground. His
restless energy saddens me
for he has what I lack:
the will to rip paths in air
and slice his mind with doing.

But I shall lie here quietly,
a soft mass yielding
to the light molding your form
and slip into shadows
until sunrise returns to our
once spoken words of heart.

xx. an afterthought

I thought I had run
out of words
about you
but warm blood and
cold air have no
finality beyond themselves.
And in the rush of work hours,
in the blare of television that
cuts through stillness
and in the liquid air
of night
you hover like the remnants
of years past
or light laced by a moving cloud
across my sky.

If I reach deep enough
I'll grasp more distance
than I care to think about
and if I cry far enough
I'll float into the future's
weightlessness
and dissolve
without a whimper.

xxi. not like falling leaves

> "And when the winds come
> I shall cry a little for the pain in them"
> *(Peter Dechert)*

But I shall sit without mourning
to watch sunlight
focus, and the sky
rain sparrows in the distance.

I think, I really think, I shall
love you always.
But if forgetfulness sets in,
let it be by permission

(Continued)

of deep shadows in the
everglades, low-lying in that
rim of memory not quite touching "gone."
And let the winds come cleanly,
not like falling leaves,
but like the drift of wild geese
sweeping on with grace.
And let our having loved
be song and dusk and late harvest
and day sounds.

    And I shall cry a little
    for the pain.

POEM EXTRACT

Your speaking
silence
floods the air
like rivers.
You haunt me
and I listen
to your eyes.

LOVE CONSIDERED

It is nice to think of love
as poetry, and you a moment.
If I were young again
and you a slim boy
kicking up the dust
on a winding country road,
love would be a half-ripe apple
plucked too soon
and I would wonder
(so would you)
why your lip trembled
like a morning daisy
while I paused to catch
the sunlight in your
hair.

SILENCE

and the thought
of your face lighting
up like a flame . . .

Wind tightens on the up-draft
The air quickens, drops
suddenly, swift
as an eagle
And brown leaves
fall like rain
Bronze earth scatters,
a shelter for small things
hugging the ground

You are without body
Your voice trails,
slipping behind hills
touching the echoing sky

Why do you turn away —
your eyes a volcano,
a despair?
Do you wait for rage
to dissemble?
Have you no answer
to give to the rising
sun?

LETTER

Your voice was disarming.
It would have been better
if you had left
without sound.

But now, as I sit here
waiting for sadness to end,
I wonder what it might
have been like never
to have known you, your eyes
rippling my skin.

There is only one way
to give love a trial:
to feather it over
like birds in flight,
to know that no song
is as sweet as your words
unspoken.

If I had it to do all
over again, I think
nothing would change —
except the way that I
tremble when sun
slants your hair
and the bend of the trees
forms an altar from
the last trace of your

shadow, lost in the
wind.

THREE LOVE POEMS

I. Love Poem

Man of mystery, power
ambition-driven
and skin of copper-gold
Some call you "dictator"
One called you "naive"
Many call you "bastard"

I reach for you
weep at night
long for your touch
You are beautiful and bright
Damn you!

You know me too well,
man of my needs
I think you must be a root-
worker, a voo doo man
crazysonofabitch!

Why do I lust for you?

II. Leaving

When I leave you
it will be like
coming into the winter
of warmth   You
have given and taken

I survive
a woman beyond grief
glad of the understanding
that hurts
A counter-sign rises
from you — place of darkness
and of light

(Continued)

The quivering mind thrusts
and cuts through granite
and when Philistines
dominate, let the spirit/
intellect carry its own
shield — a mockery
of the battle royal
falling into
ruin

III. What Matters After All

>   Smoke lifting from the
>   chimney and the sky beyond
>   take on a presence of their
>   own

Perhaps this is all that
matters, I tell myself —
the image that makes
a view, the earth,
the sky, the smell of autumn,
fire under the sun
and a cold moon
acres of darkness
and miles of crimson light

>   and the dream of you
>   outlined like a giant
>   shadow on the clear
>   white plane

ST. VALENTINE'S EVE POEM

In my season
of ghosts I wear
a crown of holes
spikes, and gold . . .
arrows of blue air.

I follow you, love
you — you with your
see-through eyes
and hands of fire.

Tomorrow is love day
and you have been my death
my basket of haves — my
sea, my plume, my breathing
craziness.

How blue is anger? How
red is pain? How
dead is good-bye?

Today is love day.
The trees, the grass
the screaming air . . .

Nothing ever stops.

MID-SUMMER THOUGHTS

> "There is silence in the sky
> The light from the hills
> lays its fingers firmly upon the hidden bones of the town."
>
> *(Major Ursa, "In Town")*

And now a moment of feeling my limbs
lying inside me like logs
on still water

Trees ascending, going
nowhere
angling towards the sky
their spreading lines
throwing patches of bronze shade
cooling me like his soft touch

The light from the hills
descends into darkness
Ivy-covered bedrock
raised against the wind

And his eyes, his smile
reaching across this band
of silent air

SPRING

Noise outside
my window —
kids playing ball —
One slithers across the grass,
yells like a cowboy.

Spring again
and the uncertain weather
brings new season . . .

Long before daybreak
I lie like a burst apple.
I straddle the night
and when the light comes,
I find a voice
in the dark hollow
of bones —
my belly a cone's shell,
my breasts pin cushions,
my ass the bride of my pillow.

Who turns the yellow dawn
to fire —
the sky a ring of striped flame
warming my body to ice? My desire
for you is a wind's draft
sweeping past the gray
and clotted silence of
thought
lost and then found in the new day's
beginning.

WHILE SITTING IN THE AIRPORT WAITING ROOM

"... because you were my love
and you matter"
    (Richard Hugo, "Letter to Kathy")

The walls are awash
with framed color:
posters that tell of New Orleans,
Miami, Chicago

A whistle
like wind syphoning
through a knothole
is only the dying cry
of a plane in port

I'll take the next flight out
The passage in
was measured at the last
weathering
Each journey clasps
like links in a chain
or raindrops at the window
buttressing glass — vertical
lines of wet alphabet
joining flight

Last winter I held you

Now I give you back to the past
and erase your memory
without passion or hate or love
or indifference, or even
a wide-eyed solitude

Where will you go
now that I release you
like no attachment to my alien
skin?

LOVE POEM

Thoughts run tonight
racing into dark corners
startle me with
their brittleness
blinding
with their insistent bright
edge

Madness propels them
over and over again —
variations on the same theme

But I will drive east
to the river at daybreak
where I have my beginnings,
will lose myself in the center
of dawn

Having roots in that place,
I will follow the streak of red
that cuts the sky
When light claims
the earth,
I will reach out and touch
your coolness invisible
without shadow
and bright as a copper coin
in sunlight

I will take you into my madness
and hold you in full bloom

SURVIVAL POEM

Her eyes were fire
and blood and wild roses
Summer was her voice
and hair her dimmest memories

He bent like autumn
touching, touching, always
touching —
a warmth bound in amber
and limbs like forests

This is a song of humanity
a survival song
a hymn of spirit
reaching across the zero line

You are you, and I am I,
folding inward, breaking forth

This is a love song
Love . . .

ABOUT THE AUTHOR

Pinkie Gordon Lane is a professor of English and departmental chairperson at Southern University in Baton Rouge, Louisiana, where she has lived since 1956. From 1974 to 1980 she was director of the annual Melvin A. Butler Black Poetry Festival sponsored by the Department, an event that brought to the campus noted poets from all over the country. A native of Philadelphia, Pennsylvania, she was educated at Spelman College, Atlanta University, and Louisiana State University, from which she was the first Black woman recipient of the Doctor of Philosophy degree.

In 1984 the author received two prestigious honors, one of which was a Baton Rouge Area YWCA award as a "Woman of Achievement." In addition, she was formally recognized as one of fifty-eight outstanding women of Louisiana; as such, she was included in the Women's Pavilion ("Women in the Mainstream") in the World Exposition held in New Orleans. In 1983 she received a national award from the Washington Chapter of the Spelman College Alumnae Association for "outstanding achievement in the area of the Arts and Humanities" for that year.

Dr. Lane has read her poetry throughout the nation, and in 1981, through the auspices of the United States International Communication Agency, visited four African countries where she read her own poetry and lectured on contemporary Afro-American women poets.

I Never Scream is this author's third volume of poetry. In addition to some new poems, it contains selections from her earlier works, *Wind Thoughts* (1972) and *The Mystic Female* (1978), the latter of which was accepted in the 1979 Pulitzer Prize for Poetry competition. Some of the poems first appeared in such periodicals as *Callaloo, Journal of Black Poetry, Ms. Magazine, Negro American Literature Forum, Nimrod, Obsidian, The Black Scholar,* and *The Southern Review.*

This collection is dedicated to her twenty-two-year-old son Gordon, a college senior majoring in jazz studies and a talented drummer who plans a career in music.

Dr. Lane sees this new volume as ". . . the search for equilibrium in a chaotic world; . . . the discovery that art is restorative; that uttering truth is not the way to become popular, but it *is* the way to become whole; that beauty, after all, is what matters, that it lifts us into the hemisphere of the spirit — our ultimate survival, our final and most profound union with our fellowman."